PRESIDING

YOU CAN DO IT!

(A GUIDE FOR ALL NEWLY ELECTED PRESIDING OFFICERS)

Second Edition

By M. Eugene Bierbaum, Ph.D., CPP-T

With Foreword by Nancy Sylvester, M.A., CPP-T

American Institute of Parliamentarians
Education Department
2014

© 2014, 2015 by American Institute of Parliamentarians
www.aipparl.org
aip@aipparl.org
888-664-0428

Produced in the United States of America
Second Edition ISBN: 978-0-942736-33-5

Second printing of the Second Edition, January 2015
2 3 4 5 6 7 8 9 10

The AIP Education Department is indebted to Kay Crews, CP, who so graciously devoted her time and talent to solving many formatting problems to produce this second edition.

Edited and Published by the
Education Department
American Institute of Parliamentarians
Jeanette N. Williams, CP-T, Education Director
Ann L. Rempel, CPP-T, Printed Materials Division Chair
Alison Wallis, JD, CP-T, President

FOREWORD

I have had the pleasure of sharing two professions with Dr. M. Eugene Bierbaum, the distinguished author of this book. We were both college communications professors who developed a love for parliamentary procedure and first met through the communications professional organization. We now have common membership in many professional organizations and frequently teach workshops together. Gene has enjoyed a tremendous level of respect from outstanding members of both professions.

This book is unique in the field of parliamentary procedure

It does not contain rules and charts but instead gives advice and guidance. From a professional parliamentarian's point of view, this book clarifies many of the concepts that we stress with our clients. From the newly elected presiding officer's point of view, this book addresses issues that often cause apprehension about the job. While this book is intended for the novice, it contains information and guidance that will be helpful for the experienced presiding officer as well.

Another unique aspect of this book is the approach to presiding as a team activity instead of an individual event. The team is defined and described and roles are clarified.

Since this book first came out, I have purchased a number of books to share with the newly elected presiding officers of organizations for which I serve as professional parliamentarian. I have also shared copies with people who are elected to leadership positions in my community; they find this book helpful in preparing for their new endeavor.

Reading this book can have a calming effect on the new presiding officer while providing the information and skills needed to preside like a professional. Gene does an outstanding job of bringing together the two professions of communications and parliamentary procedure in a way that will benefit both new and seasoned presiding officers.

Nancy Sylvester, M.A., CPP-T

M. Eugene Bierbaum received his Ph.D. in communication theory from the University of Missouri in 1965 and served as the tenth president of AIP during 1976-1978. During 1979-1983 he served as curriculum director for the first AIP Practicums offered at the College of William and Mary. He served as accrediting director during 1981-1984 and education director during 1997-2000. Following twenty-five years of teaching communication studies at the State University of New York, he retired in 1992 with the title of professor emeritus. During 1991-2001 he chaired a committee to write the Joint Code of Ethics that was subsequently adopted by the American Institute of Parliamentarians and the National Association of Parliamentarians. He continues to teach workshops on parliamentary procedure throughout the United States.

INTRODUCTION

Since the early 1970s I have been deeply involved with the two major parliamentary associations and have taught many workshops that involve presiding skills. Within the first few years of my professional involvement, however, I began to question whether we, as a profession, were teaching the right things to the right people. Two questions concerned me: (1) Why do virtually all of the parliamentary authorities begin with the assumption that the presiding officer should be an expert on parliamentary procedure? (2) Why does the profession devote so much time and energy to teaching novice parliamentarians to preside?

The first question concerned me deeply because I have never known an elected officer who qualified as an expert on parliamentary procedure either at the beginning or the end of the term of office. As I became more deeply involved in the profession, I found myself increasingly at odds with my fellow parliamentarians regarding the proper role of the presiding officer. Finally, in 1978, I wrote an article specifically repudiating the notion that any elected presiding officer should be an expert on parliamentary procedure. The article, entitled "The Role of the Presiding Officer" appeared in the April issue of the Parliamentary Journal and was later republished in Gregg Phifer's Readings in Parliamentary Law (AIP, Kendall Hunt Publishing Co., 1992). That article has remained my guiding philosophy, and provides the background for this work on presiding.

My basic viewpoint in this book is that the elected presiding officer provides critical leadership in the areas of membership and organizational issues and goals. To be effective in this leadership role, the presiding officer must not become distracted by rules and procedures. Viewed from this perspective, any presiding officer who attempts to be a membership expert, an organizational expert, and a procedural expert (i.e., emphasis on rule books, charts of motions, etc.) is simply attempting to do too much, and runs a high risk that none of the various roles will be performed satisfactorily.

This book emphasizes the inherent strengths of the elected presiding officer, and points the way toward maximum development and fulfillment of the presiding officer's leadership potential. The underlying assumption, which stands in direct contradiction to most rulebooks, is that elected presiding officers cannot and should not focus on rules and procedures during their term of office. Rather, they should develop their leadership potential by focusing entirely on the membership and the attainment of organizational goals and objectives. How one can maintain this focus while at the same time coping with complex rules and procedures is the subject of this book.

My second concern is whether the parliamentary profession is training its future parliamentarians correctly. Why do we spend so much time teaching them presiding skills when only a few of them will ever preside? Why are we not doing more to help the novice parliamentarian adjust to an advisory role and become an effective member of the presiding "team"? Since this book focuses on the needs of elected presiding officers, I have chosen not to digress into the question of how parliamentarians should be trained. This question, which has been largely ignored by the profession, deserves a book of its own.

ACKNOWLEDGEMENTS

Ann Rempel and Mary Randolph, who invited me to write the first edition of this book, and Jeanette Williams and Ann Rempel, who urged me to produce this second edition, know how much I despise writing. They know that I am more comfortable teaching a class than sitting in front of my computer. I am grateful for their insistence that I separate myself from the teaching environment long enough to address the needs of thousands of elected presiding officers. Also, I wish to thank Nancy Sylvester for sharing her professional insights with me as the writing progressed.

My profound hope is that this book will find its way into the hands of the newly elected presiding officer who doesn't have a clue about where to begin. If I can help such a person develop a highly focused approach to presiding and attain maximum leadership potential for the organization, then I will have realized a lifelong dream.

CONTENTS

Who me?
Preside?!

Chapter 1
Why You Hate Presiding

Congratulations! You have now achieved your lifelong dream of being elected to the highest office in your organization, the office of president. Perhaps you have been chosen to serve as chair of the assembly, or maybe you hold the position of vice president with specific responsibilities to preside. Whatever your position, you, as presiding officer, will be the occupant of "the chair," and all eyes will be on you.

It is no accident that everyone will be looking in your direction. If your organization uses any semblance of parliamentary procedure during business meetings, one of the most basic rules is that all communication flows to and from the chair. In other words, no one can speak without your permission and, when they speak, they must speak directly to the chair, not to some other member in the room.

So, you will control the meeting. You draft the agenda for the meeting, you call the meeting to order, you call for the reading of the minutes, you make your report as president, you call on all other officers and committees to make their reports, you are in charge during the handling of unfinished business and new business, and you, and only you, can adjourn the meeting. Why are you complaining? You are in the spotlight. You are the elected star of the show!

The truth is that few people really want the responsibility of being in charge of an organization. You have just accepted a responsibility that will interfere with your private life and will require you to reassess your priorities. You may have to occasionally forego a social function to do your job. At the end of a hard day's work, you will have more work to do. The people whom you are trying to please will sometimes be displeased, and sometimes display ingratitude. Yet, these factors barely scratch the surface of why you hate presiding.

Before we try to solve your presiding problem, let's take a look at why you really don't want to do this. The reasons will vary among different presiding officers, but you are bound to find that at least one of the following fits your situation perfectly.

You *really, really hate* presiding because —

I hate presiding because
I'm scared

Fear of speaking in public has always been a number one cause of fear. It is said that some people actually fear speaking in public more than they fear death. Whether or not this is true in your case, the fact is that you will be doing lots of speaking in public, and, unless your organization has a well-paid staff to assist you, you will do most of your speaking "off the cuff," that is, without a script to assist you.

Most people hate public speaking because they dread the possibility of making a disastrous mistake in the public arena. Suppose you open the meeting with the words, "The meeting will now be adjourned." You have just made an absolute fool of yourself, and everyone in the room knows it. But such things have happened, and they will undoubtedly happen again.

The fact that you know most or all of the people in the room doesn't make your job any easier, it only multiplies the fear that you already feel. Why should you fear these people? These are the people who elected you to the office that you now hold. In many cases, these people have been your friends for years. But, you have become accustomed to communicating with them on a one-on-one basis, or in small groups. Now, you are coming face to face with them in an entirely different situation. You are standing up front, and they are all sitting down looking at you. How nice if they could all be strangers; then you wouldn't have to worry so much about making a complete fool of yourself.

There is, of course, a simple solution to this fear factor. It's called having a sense of humor. You were not elected to this office because you never make mistakes. You were elected to do a job, and, of course, some mistakes will occur. Members will not hate you just because you make an occasional mistake, as long as they feel secure that you are doing the best you can with your new job. Learn to laugh at yourself occasionally. When you goof, it can be an occasion for everyone to relax and laugh a bit (they are laughing *with* you, not *at* you). Laugh at yourself, too. People will love you for it, and the entire meeting will be more relaxed and amiable.

Another thing that will help is simple practice. If you have never done much speaking in public, practice in front of a family member or a few friends. Try to "see" a larger audience, and practice speaking to them just as you would during a business meeting. "Practice makes perfect" is a good rule to follow, as long as you are willing to admit to an occasional honest mistake.

As you practice, get used to watching the reactions of your audience, and respond to those reactions. People like to feel that they count for something, and that you actually care about them. If you think you sense confusion, disagreement, or hostility, don't continue with your prepared speech. Stop, and try to figure out what the problem is. If something you said wasn't clear, give another example. If you said something that evoked strong disagreement, maybe you need to rephrase your statement.

If you practice in the manner described above, you will gradually evolve from "I-centered" speaking to "audience-centered" speaking. Public speaking that is focused mainly on the reactions of the audience rather than on your own inner fears will be much more readily accepted and much more effective in the long run. Remember that these people in front of you voted for you; they are your supporters as well as your audience, and they want you to do well. All you have to do is make an honest effort.

I hate presiding because
I don't understand the rulebooks

Congratulations! You have now joined the ranks of millions of others who haven't the faintest idea of what the rulebooks (often referred to as "parliamentary authorities") actually say. If it makes you feel any better, you should understand that rulebooks are often written by lawyers, and, as everyone knows, lawyers do not always write in user-friendly language. Some rulebooks, people have argued, appear to be written *by* lawyers *for* lawyers. But, you will still need some basic rules for your meetings, and ignorance is no excuse. So, what should you do?

First of all, you need to find out which rules your organization has adopted. These rules are contained in your corporate charter (if your organization is incorporated), your constitution and bylaws (these may be combined into one document called *bylaws*), and any standing rules and special rules of order that your organization has adopted. These documents should routinely be available to all members, but you may have to search for them. The organization's rules may have been ignored for years, but you need to find out which rules should be followed, and follow them.

In your search for rules, you may discover that your organization has adopted the latest edition of *Robert's Rules of Order Newly Revised* which is the parliamentary authority most commonly used by voluntary associations in the United States. Many other parliamentary authorities are available, however, and some organizations have adopted *American Institute of Parliamentarians Standard Code of Parliamentary Procedure*, *Demeter's Manual of Parliamentary Law and Procedure*, *Cannon's Concise Guide to Rules of Order*, or other books of rules. The bylaws will tell you which parliamentary authority contains the official rules of your organization.

Whatever rules your organization has adopted are the rules that you will have to follow. Knowing and following those rules is part of your job description. If the members don't understand the rules that they have adopted, part of your job is to educate them on how to use the rules properly.

Learning the rules and educating your membership to follow the rules may sound like a daunting job for someone who has never even read a rulebook. This job, however, is not yours alone. You will have a team to help you. Later chapters will tell you how to assemble your presiding team and how to use this team effectively.

So, don't give up yet. Read on.

I hate presiding because
I can't speak the language of parliamentary procedure

Now we're getting down to the gut-level fears that all presiding officers have. Presiding is not just a matter of doing public speaking. You can't solve all of your problems by manifesting a sense of humor and learning to laugh at your own mistakes. You might even be tempted to use the worst solution of all — to blame your problems on parliamentary procedure. Don't do this. This is one fatal mistake that some presiding officers make — they can't accept blame, so they blame the rules. Remember that someone had to adopt these rules in the first place, and the rules have to be followed.

We are concerned with much more than just public speaking, and much more than simply following rules. To preside effectively, you need to speak the language of parliamentary procedure, and there's no way around this. Learning to speak the language of parliamentary procedure is very much like learning a foreign language. You must not only learn it, but you must *use* it on a regular basis.

Chapter 10, "Speaking the Language," will help you get started. Regardless of which parliamentary authority your organization has adopted, there are certain refinements of language that you will have to get used to. Such a simple thing as speaking in the third person (i.e., "The chair recognizes the member") is not an easy task for everyone. You will also need to develop proper language for adopting your agenda, approving minutes, calling for reports, receiving and approving reports, handling unfinished and new business, and other procedural matters.

Once again, the solution is *practice*. Your first meeting will likely be your toughest. Gradually, you will learn to communicate with your membership in the language of parliamentary procedure. Don't expect to develop this skill overnight. It takes both time and practice. Eventually, you will feel comfortable with it.

But, Can I Preside?

Yes, you can. So far, we have discussed the reasons that people most commonly give when asked why they hate presiding. They fear public speaking, they don't understand the rules, and they don't speak the language. But you, as the elected presiding officer, have many hidden assets of which you may not be aware. You are probably much better qualified to preside than most of your members. The following chapter will discuss the true nature of presiding, and you may be surprised to find that your job description is much different than you thought. Once you understand what is expected of you, and what is not expected, you will come to see that

Yes, You Can Preside

Chapter 2
You Can Preside

Think about why you were elected to your position. How were you selected? Were there other candidates for the position? Did you have to campaign for election? Did you make any promises, or declare your goals for the organization before you were elected? In some cases, the answer to these questions is affirmative, but in many other cases the job fell to you because nobody else wanted it. Regardless of how you got here, however, the point is that the organization needs you and they have placed their trust in you. They want to know your goals, both short term and long term, and they want to help you reach those goals. If you were duly elected by majority vote, you have a mandate to perform for the organization.

What, exactly, do you think the membership expects of you? Did they elect you because you are an expert on parliamentary procedure? Did they elect you because of your superior public speaking skills? Did they elect you because you always have the right words on the tip of your tongue to speak the language of meetings in precisely the right way? The answer to all of these questions, of course, is NO! You were not elected for any of these reasons.

Officers are elected because they are known and appreciated by the membership. No one understands the membership better than the elected officers. The president, especially, is the one who knows all the inside workings of the organization. The president knows the history of the organization, where points of tension exist, where factions exist, and which members belong to which factions. The president knows that whenever one member stands to speak, certain other members, who are also known by name to the president, will almost always oppose this member.

The presiding officer, usually the president, understands the strengths and weaknesses of the organization. The presiding officer understands the direction that the organization needs to go, and the obstacles that may stand in the way. The presiding officer understands the basic financial status of the organization, its membership base, and its relationship to similar organizations. There is a good chance that the presiding officer has served on the board of directors, or at least on certain key committees of the organization. If the organization is large and powerful, the presiding officer may have inside information on certain legal problems that the organization has faced in the past and may encounter again.

In short, your true expertise as presiding officer lies not in your public speaking ability, nor in your knowledge of the rules, nor in your ability to speak proper parliamentary language. Your expertise is that of the organizational expert. The presiding officer knows the organization inside out, and this field of specialized knowledge will be a source of constant support whenever you preside over a meeting. Members are willing to overlook a multitude of errors as long as they feel confidence in the basic leadership of their elected officers.

The job of the presiding officer is to facilitate communication among members

Since you are one of the most knowledgeable people around regarding the organization's membership and goals, you are the one in the best position to facilitate communication within the body. And, you don't need a book of rules to do this. Your job is not limited to presiding over motions that may be introduced during a meeting; your job is to preside over the communication that occurs at all levels throughout the business meeting. Consider how much knowledge you have in each of the following areas, all of which are legitimate concerns for the presiding officer.

1. The presiding officer is familiar with all of the cliques and factions present during the meeting. You can often identify, in advance, how certain groups are likely to vote on sensitive motions. You know why the factions were organized, their history, and most of their strategies for getting their way.

2. The presiding officer can identify any hidden agenda that is likely to dominate a meeting. Because you know the membership so well, you know that members do not always speak openly about their true feelings on controversial matters, and you are in the best position to quickly identify any member who is grandstanding.

3. The presiding officer is familiar with customs and traditions, and how these may affect business to come before the assembly. Customs in some organizations are so firmly entrenched that they sometimes carry more weight than standard rules of procedure. For example, most parliamentary authorities require nominations from the floor prior to any election. The president may follow this rule by calling for nominations from the floor. Custom, however, may dictate that no nominations from the floor will ever be forthcoming. In some organizations, the longstanding tradition is that the slate recommended by the nominating committee is elected by acclamation.

4. The presiding officer understands the protocol of the organization. Each organization has its own protocol, and no book of rules will help much in this area. You, as presiding officer, are in the best position to deal with protocol. When should guests be seated on the platform? When should they be seated with the voting membership, and when, if ever, should they be segregated from the voting membership? How are deceased members to be honored? Which reports should be highlighted as being of vital importance to the organization, and how should they be highlighted? Which members should be recognized for outstanding service to the organization, and how should this recognition be conferred? The presiding officer is often in the best position to decide these and many other matters of protocol.

The list could go on and on. The point, however, is that you were elected to serve as the organization's expert on the organization and its membership. Your job, while presiding, is to facilitate communication among the membership in such a way that you help them to make important decisions affecting the organization and its goals. Your attention, while presiding, will not be on rules, but on the members, the issues, the cliques and factions, how things are going for the organization, and how things should be going for the organization.

If your attention is where it should be, on the membership and the issues, you won't have much time for intricate rules and procedures. When a motion is introduced in a meeting, you won't have much time to reflect on whether a second is required, whether the motion is amendable and/or debatable, and what kind of vote is required to adopt the motion. Your attention is, and should be on the substance of the motion, where it came from, its intent, and what effect it will have on the organization if adopted.

Your approach to presiding, if you are to be effective, must be very disciplined. Keep your focus where it belongs at all times: on the membership, the organization, and the goals of the organization. Do not allow yourself to be distracted by anything else while you are presiding. You can preside effectively if you keep the focus of your attention where it belongs. You are the organization's expert on matters of organizational substance, and you understand the membership better than anyone else. Hence, you are the most qualified person to do this job.

Having said all of this, certain questions must be arising in your mind. If I keep my focus on the membership and the substantive issues that come before the meeting, how am I going to deal with the rules? What will I do if someone starts waving a rulebook in the air, claiming that we are not following proper rules?

What if I can't keep track of members that have spoken several times and others that have not spoken at all? What if several versions of a motion are introduced, and everyone is confused about which motion we are dealing with? What if a member becomes noisy and disruptive? What happens if a faction walks out and we lose our quorum? What is a "quorum" anyway, and how does it affect our meeting? And, worst of all, suppose somebody asks a question about the substance of a motion, and I go blank and can't answer the question. How can I keep my focus on the issues when I am constantly being distracted by all of these other things?

If you allow yourself to be distracted by all of these questions, you will panic and you will be unable to preside effectively. Your problem now is that you are going it alone, and there is no need for you to do this. Presiding was never meant to be a one-person job. You will be able to preside effectively only after you accept that you are only one member (the central, most important member, to be sure, but still just one member) of a team.

Presiding is a team effort. An important part of your job, therefore, is to surround yourself with an effective presiding team. The choices that you make in assembling your presiding team will have profound effects on the entire term of your presidency. Therefore, take you time and choose wisely.

Yes, You Can Preside
But
You Need a Team to Help You Do It

This rule applies to everyone who presides over meetings, large or small. Even professional parliamentarians who preside cannot go it alone. Presiding was never meant to be a one-person show.

This page intentionally left blank.

Chapter 3
Selecting a Parliamentarian

When you were first elected to the office of president, probably the last thing that entered your mind was finding a parliamentarian. You had quite a list of important priorities ahead of the parliamentarian, didn't you? Perhaps the idea of hiring or appointing a parliamentarian had never even entered your mind. You just assumed that parliamentarians were only for very large conventions, only for writing bylaws, or only for occasional use when something big, like a major dues increase, was pending. Think again. Every meeting requires a parliamentarian and, if you have read the preceding chapters carefully, you should by this time understand your need for someone with specialization in meeting procedures.

Presiding, as we have noted, is not a one-person job. The presiding officer is, and should be, entirely focused on the substance of the meeting, the membership, and the issues. What you are looking for now is a person who will be entirely focused in the opposite direction. All of the things that you have been blissfully ignoring in order to stay properly focused as a presiding officer must become the central focus of another person who sits beside you and watches nothing but procedures.

You do not have to know a lot about rules of order. The person sitting next to you, the parliamentarian, has studied them carefully and is prepared to give you advice on any procedural issue that may arise. The parliamentarian is the one who advises you, if necessary, that other main motions cannot be introduced while a main motion is pending for action. Many strange types of motions that you have never heard of may suddenly interrupt the flow of your meeting (for example, reconsider and enter on the minutes, previous question, demand for a quorum count, lay on the table, and other motions).

If you were trying to do everything yourself, you would be responsible to know how to handle any type of motion that might be made during the meeting. You would have to respond to all parliamentary inquiries (questions about procedure), make rulings from the chair without any assistance, and attempt to resolve all procedural disputes. Do you think you could handle all of that? A few brave souls have tried, and very few have succeeded.

Some parliamentary authorities claim that the presiding officer should know more about parliamentary procedure than any other member. Respectfully, I disagree. You were not elected because of your knowledge of parliamentary procedure. If you want to study it and develop some basic skills of handling motions on your own, fine; but this will be a difficult task for some otherwise well qualified presiding officers. Some people learn parliamentary procedure more quickly than others, in the same way that some people learn foreign languages more easily than others. Your knowledge, or lack thereof, should not be the measure of your success or failure as a presiding officer.

The main point is that you, as presiding officer, need not be especially skilled in parliamentary procedure, but it is essential that your presiding team include a parliamentarian who is, by definition, a specialist in meeting procedures. Please note that not everyone is well suited to this job. How many people do you know who are willing to sit through a meeting watching nothing but procedures? This requires special training. Finding the right person to do this job will, to a very large degree, determine the success or failure of business meetings conducted during your term of office.

Searching for a Parliamentarian

Where do you go to find a parliamentarian? One solution is to contact the American Institute of Parliamentarians (AIP) and ask for recommendations. AIP will provide names of certified parliamentarians in your geographic area. Before you make this contact, however, you need to find out if your organization has the resources to interview candidates and hire a certified parliamentarian. If you do not have the resources, then you must utilize other means.

The Member Parliamentarian

Probably the most common method of appointing a parliamentarian is to simply appoint one of your own members. Great care must be exercised, however, if you use this option. This member, if not already skilled in the field of parliamentary procedure, will have to find some way to master at least the basics of the field. AIP offers at least two practicums each year for interactive training in parliamentary procedure. If the person cannot afford to attend workshops or practicums, courses may be taken by correspondence. AIP offers a variety of correspondence courses by mail and through the Internet. Another possibility is that a university or college campus near you may offer a class in parliamentary procedure. Refer to Chapter 10 for further information on workshops and correspondence courses.

Taking a course in parliamentary procedure, however, is not the only requirement to become a parliamentarian. This person will be forfeiting virtually all of the rights usually associated with membership, except for the right to attend meetings. Your parliamentarian will not be able to enter into debate on any subject, and will not be able to vote except when a vote is conducted by ballot. Furthermore, the parliamentarian will be obligated to adopt a complete detachment from all of the various issues that confront your organization. This person will be concerned only with following proper procedures, and must never give any evidence of favoring or disfavoring a particular position. Your best bet might be to look for a relatively new member with no apparent aspirations to higher office. Another possibility would be an older member who has held a variety of offices in the association and is nearing retirement.

Your choice of a parliamentarian should be based on two major criteria. The person you select (a) must have at least a basic knowledge of the field of parliamentary procedure, and (b) must at all times maintain a clear focus on procedures, never on issues or members. This is not an easy task for any member of your organization, especially for anyone who is deeply involved in organizational issues. Hence, you want to go outside of your organization for a parliamentarian if you can possibly find a way to do so.

Other Options

If you lack the resources to hire a professional parliamentarian, and if you think that the member parliamentarian is not a good idea for your organization, there are other options that you may wish to explore. You may find members of AIP living in your area (again, you could contact

AIP Headquarters for this information) who are preparing to become certified parliamentarians. Parliamentarians in training are often willing to donate their services to gain experience in the field.

Another option would be to actively recruit someone in your community (not a member of your organization) to join AIP, order appropriate educational literature, and get into some type of training program. Early retirees looking for a way to fill their time are a good bet for this type of training. Keep in mind, however, that the person who trains for your organization might later wish to start working for other organizations as well, and might begin charging fees.

Regardless of which way you choose to go about finding a parliamentarian, do not neglect to fulfill this important task. If you attempt to run a meeting without someone to assist you in matters of procedure, you will quickly find yourself in over your head. You don't want to be standing up there trying to work through a complex issue of considerable importance to your organization when somebody suddenly throws a strange motion at you. You won't know what to do, and neither will anybody else in the room.

This is not written to frighten you, but you should understand that one of the main reasons that parliamentarians get hired is to deal with unruly members who often make strange and unheard of motions. If someone stands up in the middle of a meeting and starts waving around a book of rules, claiming to know everything in it, there is no substitute for having a professional right there on the spot to quote chapter and verse and help bring things back to order.

Some professional parliamentarians have taken the position that they refuse to be hired by an organization that has waited until things got "out of hand." They don't want to be put in the position of having to clean up the mess that was made by somebody else. They want to be hired early enough that they can prevent serious procedural problems from developing.

You, as the organization's presiding officer, also cannot afford to wait until a serious problem develops. The time to start looking for a parliamentarian is the day you are elected. If you put it off, or entirely neglect this important duty, your presidency will likely suffer irreparable damage long before your term ends.

If you have been elected presiding officer, or if you anticipate your possible election in the near future, begin now to figure out how you are going to find this important person, the parliamentarian, who sits beside you, watches nothing but procedures, and is always there to help you out of a tight spot. You will sleep much easier at night, and you will quickly develop confidence that, with your parliamentarian's help,

You Can Preside

This page intentionally left blank.

Chapter 4
Working with Your Parliamentarian

Once you have selected your parliamentarian, you must now develop a working relationship with this person. The exact nature of this relationship will vary widely from one organization to another, depending partly on the temperaments of the presiding officer and the parliamentarian, the size and scope of the organization, and the particular demands of the presiding situation.

Where to Put Your Parliamentarian

Your first concern should be where to place your parliamentarian. If you have a head table, it is best to have the parliamentarian seated at this table directly next to the presiding officer's lectern. You want to have the person physically as close to you as is practical because the parliamentarian's advice must often be given quickly and quietly while an important issue is under discussion. The parliamentarian will normally give advice only to you, not to the assembly, while the meeting is in progress. If the parliamentarian is seated a distance from you, or if some other person sits between you and the parliamentarian, the advice may come too late.

If you know that you hear better in one ear than the other, place the parliamentarian next to your good ear. The assembly will rarely, if ever, hear this person speak. To the members, the parliamentarian often appears to be sitting up there doing nothing. But you, as presiding officer, know that this person is a specialist that you cannot do without.

The Beginner Parliamentarian

If your parliamentarian is a relative beginner, you will need to clarify the role that this person is to perform during meetings. Carefully explain that the parliamentarian may never discuss any issue, even to provide information, and may never vote unless he is a member — and then only in the case of a ballot vote. Also, be sure that this person understands that at no point will the parliamentarian ever be in charge of the meeting. This person will never address the membership unless you, as presiding officer, make a specific request for this kind of assistance.

Getting Parliamentary Advice

You need to make some arrangement with your parliamentarian regarding how and when procedural advice is to be communicated to you. Experienced parliamentarians often give advice to the presiding officer while members' attention is directed toward a speaker. It is usually best not to restrict your parliamentarian to responding only to your direct questions. Many parliamentarians are highly skilled in anticipating procedural problems, and they can often advise you about what they see coming up that could cause problems. Indeed, the best parliamentarians are proactive, although they may not appear so to the membership, in anticipating and dealing with procedural problems before they come to the floor.

Card Systems

Some parliamentarians have developed card systems for giving advice. A green card, for example, might signify that a particular motion is in order, whereas a red card signifies that it is out of order. Certain cards, discretely displayed only to the presiding officer, might tell you whether a motion requires a second, is debatable, is amendable, and what kind of vote is required. The most important card, perhaps a psychedelic orange, says, "Stop. We need to talk now." When this happens, simply tell the membership that you need a moment to consult with your parliamentarian.

Many parliamentarians prefer to work without a card system. They will sometimes whisper their advice to the presiding officer, and sometimes will pass notes quietly and unobtrusively. The technique of whispering advice is especially useful for presiding officers who are not skilled in speaking the language of parliamentary procedure. The parliamentarian's advice may often contain the exact words that should be repeated by the presiding officer to the assembly. Word-for-word advice on what to say next is especially important when dealing with highly technical matters such as a substitute motion or an appeal from the decision of the chair.

Occasionally a presiding officer, caught up in the midst of a heated argument, will ignore the parliamentarian. This is not usually done intentionally. The presiding officer simply gets too absorbed in what the members are saying, and the parliamentarian is unable to get the attention of the presiding officer at the critical moment that the advice is most needed. Try to develop a habit of always listening to your parliamentarian. Don't fall into the trap of thinking that the substantive issues of the moment are more important than mere parliamentary procedure. Your parliamentarian is a valuable resource, and you ignore this person at your own peril. When your parliamentarian needs to talk to you, stop and listen.

Pacing the Meeting

The most important advice for any new presiding officer is never to allow yourself to be rushed while presiding. If you need time to clear your head, consult with your parliamentarian, or consult with anyone else at the head table, take the time to do it. If someone makes a motion that is ambiguous and confusing, do not be rushed into discussion of the motion. Let your parliamentarian look at it first. The best advice might be to send the motion back to the maker, not to change the intent of the motion, but to clarify the language. Nothing confuses the membership more than a poorly worded, lengthy, ambiguous motion. Under certain circumstances, a brief recess might calm things down. You must maintain control of the meeting at all times, and this includes how you pace the meeting.

Occasionally members may demand a "ruling" from the parliamentarian, but this is no reason for you to relinquish control of the meeting. Parliamentarians cannot make rulings. You should inform the members that the parliamentarian is an adviser, and is not in charge of running the meeting. If the members need advice about procedures, the questions must come to you, and you should provide the answers. You may, of course, consult with the parliamentarian before responding to a question. The important thing is that you retain control of the meeting at all times. Occasionally, you may wish to call on the parliamentarian to explain a particularly complex procedural matter to the membership (for example, just before an important ballot vote). You should not do this very often, however, lest you weaken the image of leadership that is so vitally important to your position.

A well-trained parliamentarian always strives to "make the presiding officer look good." The parliamentarian gives the right advice at the right time and does it in such a way that the presiding officer always appears to be in firm control of the meeting. The parliamentarian helps the presiding officer to phrase rulings in such a way that members are not offended and actively assists the presiding officer in the correct use of parliamentary language. At the end of the meeting, if the parliamentarian has done a good job, the presiding officer will receive all of the credit for having run an excellent meeting.

Getting the Most from your Parliamentarian

If you are fortunate enough to be able to hire an experienced, professional parliamentarian, you have a valuable resource that should not be wasted. Part of your job is to ensure that you use this person's unique skills to maximum advantage.

Here are a few tips to ensure appropriate use of your parliamentarian.

1. Include the parliamentarian "in the loop" at the earliest possible time. Some presiding officers make the mistake of not involving the parliamentarian until a few days prior to the meeting. Actually, the parliamentarian can be of great assistance in drafting the notice of the meeting, especially if bylaw amendments are involved. How meetings are noticed is a critical part of your preparation, and parliamentarians know exactly what must be included in the notice.

2. Don't limit your parliamentarian's attendance to large membership meetings. Small preparatory meetings are often just as important, if not more important than the convention or annual meeting. The parliamentarian should usually attend the board meeting preceding any convention. The parliamentarian may often be of service to a bylaws committee, a rules committee, or other key standing committees of your organization.

3. Scripting meetings, or at least portions of meetings, in advance is an excellent practice because the script provides specific language for the presiding officer. Involve your parliamentarian

both in writing the script and in the practice review session. Script review sessions are one of your best preparatory tools for a successful meeting, and the parliamentarian should always be present at these sessions.

4. During annual meetings or conventions, it is helpful to establish "parliamentarian hours" when members and factions can come to the parliamentarian for assistance. The parliamentarian can often help write motions and can also advise regarding the placement of the motion on the agenda.

5. Most importantly, don't fail to involve your parliamentarian in the education of your membership. Many parliamentarians are highly skilled at teaching parliamentary workshops. If well taught, these workshops can be both entertaining and informative. Other parliamentarians have written parliamentary handbooks or regular columns of parliamentary advice for publication in the organization's newsletter. A well-educated membership will make your job as presiding officer much easier.

This page intentionally left blank.

Chapter 5
The Complete Presiding Team

You and your parliamentarian are the key members of the presiding team. Your job is to focus on the membership and the issues; the parliamentarian focuses solely on procedures. But, most presiding officers have an expanded team that includes other members. The minimum expanded team required for most organizations consists of your elected officers and a timer. Each member of the team performs a unique function.

The President-elect (or Vice President)

You probably have never thought of this person as part of your presiding team. But, if you become ill or miss a meeting for any reason whatever, the officer specified in the bylaws will be presiding in your place. You therefore need to keep this person updated on important issues to come before the organization. Also, in the event that you ever wish to "vacate the chair" to speak and vote on issues that you feel are especially vital to the organization, this person will occupy the chair. Treat this person as an important part of your team — you never know when he or she will be needed.

The Secretary

The secretary keeps the minutes and may also be in charge of official correspondence for the organization. You must learn to work with this person because you are dependent on the secretary to provide an accurate record of what is decided in the meeting.

Occasionally presiding officers will try to write their own notes in meetings, keeping records of pending motions, counts of votes taken, and/or a record of motions that were adopted. The best presiding officers, however, do little or no writing during a meeting. If there is any doubt about the exact wording of a motion under consideration, the presiding officer calls on the secretary to read the motion. If a roll call vote is required, the task of calling out the roll may be assigned to the secretary.

The secretary's most important single task is to keep accurate minutes of the meeting. The minutes don't tell you what was said during the meeting, but they do tell you what was decided and what actions were taken. You need this information to make up the agenda for the next meeting. The minutes will tell you what committees need to report, who was responsible for taking follow-up action on anything that was decided, and what business, if any, was postponed to the next meeting or left unfinished.

If your secretary is unskilled in taking minutes, your parliamentarian should be able to help with the instruction of the temporary secretary. You may have to impress upon your secretary the importance of having accurate minutes. These are the official records of the organization, and they provide a permanent record of what occurred during your term of office.

The Treasurer

You will not refer to the treasurer and/or finance committee as often as some of your other advisers, but occasionally financial advice is needed during a meeting. Members often want to know how much something costs or how money is being spent. Before adopting a motion, they may want a cost estimate for the proposed action. You, as presiding officer, are not expected to have this information on the tip of your tongue. You do, however, need to know when to defer to your treasurer and/or finance chair for the appropriate advice.

The Timer

Almost all meetings need someone to keep time; otherwise, meetings can go on "forever." A good presiding officer will try to ensure that meetings do not run overtime. Members tend to stay away from meetings that run too long.

A common practice is to limit the number of minutes that a speaker may talk. In large conventions, the limit may be as short as one or two minutes. In larger groups, the limit could be as long as five or ten minutes.

In addition to limiting the number of minutes per speech, large conventions frequently limit the total amount of time that can be spent on any one issue. For example, the total time, including all amendments, points of order, and other procedural motions may be limited to thirty minutes. If the assembly adopts this rule, all pending questions automatically come to a vote at the end of the specified time limit.

For large meetings and conventions, your team may be further expanded to include a number of staff positions. Most of this expanded team will consist of employees hired by your executive director. In some organizations, the executive director also hires the parliamentarian. In very large organizations, the executive director functions as a coordinator of a headquarters office where the board of directors and key committees meet, training programs are conducted, records of membership and dues are kept, correspondence is mailed out, scripts for meetings are prepared, and many other functions are performed to make your job easier. Don't be intimidated by your headquarters staff. You are still the presiding officer and the staff exists to make your job easier.

The Executive Director

Only the largest organizations have executive directors, and yours may not have one. If, however, you do have an executive director, this person frequently has the latest information about what is happening in the headquarters office. Executive directors often present their own reports to the membership. Still, members sometimes ask questions of the presiding officer that can only be answered by the executive director. In large organizations, it is common practice for the parliamentarian to sit on one side of the presiding officer's lectern, and the executive director on the other side. In such cases, both the parliamentarian and the executive director must be careful to give advice only when it is needed. It is possible to confuse a presiding officer with too much advice. The presiding officer looks to the parliamentarian for advice on procedural matters and to the executive director on matters of substance. Take your time, listen, and if the advice becomes too overwhelming, take a break. The membership can wait for a minute or two while you get the necessary advice. Proceed with business only when you feel ready.

The Attorney

Large associations often hire an attorney who advises on all matters involving legal documents and issues. Attorneys frequently do not attend meetings, but are available for consultation between meetings. Occasionally it is helpful for them to attend meetings when members want to hear an explanation of a complex legal issue. When they attend, attorneys usually sit at a separate table and are called upon only when legal issues arise. A runner may be used to get messages delivered between the attorney and the presiding officer.

The Spotter

The "spotter" is usually a member of the staff in large organizations. In smaller organizations, the parliamentarian or the presiding officer may assume this role. The spotter's function is to determine the order in which speakers are to be recognized by the chair. This function is particularly important in large conventions where speakers must get to microphones to speak, and a number of speakers may be lined up at each microphone waiting to speak. Many times a special microphone is designated for raising points of order and points of information. The spotter watches the order in which speakers approach the various microphones and provides the presiding officer with numbered cards indicating the order in which the various microphones are to be recognized.

Spotters are generally not used in small meetings. If necessary, the parliamentarian can assist in advising the chair about the order in which speakers were seeking recognition. If necessary, the parliamentarian could also keep a running tab on which speakers have spoken to a particular issue. This enables the presiding officer to recognize all speakers who have not spoken before recognizing anyone a second time.

Runners

Members of the staff are sometimes assigned to "run" completed motion forms between the business table (described below) and the presiding officer. Runners are also used to get messages back and forth to key members during meetings. During large conventions especially, it's handy to have one or two runners available to get messages back and forth while you are presiding.

Microphone Monitors

Where speakers must approach a microphone to speak, it is wise to have a monitor at each microphone. The monitor will often assist in gaining the presiding officer's attention. The monitor may provide motion forms on which members can write their motions. Sometimes monitors will be assigned to raise colored cards indicating whether the member is speaking for the pending motion, against the pending motion, or wishes to propose a new motion such as an amendment.

Floor Managers

The specific composition of the presiding team will vary greatly from one organization to another. A major factor is the hiring of staff, which can vary from zero to a very large, diversified professional staff. Some organizations with limited staff appoint members as floor managers. Member floor managers may perform any or all of the following duties, as assigned by the presiding officer:

1. Assist other members in writing motions.
2. Line up speakers for debate, alternating between affirmative and negative speakers.
3. Distribute colored cards (green to speak for, red to speak against, white to ask a question, and so forth).
4. Keep up-to-date lists of nominees for office.

Other Staff

At large conventions, a business table is generally maintained near the dais. Many functions are performed here, such as distribution of motion forms, distribution of materials to microphone monitors, and distribution of minutes and announcements. The timer, the executive director, and other staff may be seated at this table. Counted votes may be tabulated at this table and the results conveyed to the presiding officer.

In addition to the salaried staff, you may occasionally find it necessary to appoint special committees as part of your presiding team. If frequent votes are to be taken, you may need to appoint a tellers committee. If you wish to monitor members entering and leaving the room during meetings, you may need the help of a sergeant-at-arms committee.

Your job, as presiding officer, is to understand the function of each member of your team, and know when and how to use them. If you need procedural advice, consult your parliamentarian. If someone raises a question about headquarters operations, refer the question to the executive director. If a legal question arises, consult with the attorney. Watch your timer's signals, which are agreed upon in advance, to know when you should stop speakers or bring a pending motion to an immediate vote. If you need a motion in writing, or need quick information from individual members while business is pending, use your runners. Eventually you will develop a team that works together smoothly, and you may actually start to enjoy your job as presiding officer.

Chapter 6
Basic Presiding: Preparing for the Meeting

You might consider this the hard part, actually learning some parliamentary procedure. Why should you need this, you may ask, if you have a qualified parliamentarian at your side to help with procedures? If you take the time to master a few basic concepts, however, you will be a better presiding officer and a more effective member of your presiding team.

Your first task is to prepare thoroughly for each meeting. Meetings that have had little or no preliminary planning will almost surely fail. Your job, as presiding officer, is to identify the issues that must be addressed, ensure that the members who are most concerned with those issues receive a fair hearing, and then allow the members to decide the issue through a fair vote. If you do your job right, you will likely spend more time planning for the meeting than actually running the meeting.

To prepare properly, you will need to perform five tasks prior to each meeting: (1) review the minutes of the prior meeting, (2) contact key members and committees, (3) prepare an agenda, (4) meet with your parliamentarian, and (5) prepare your team.

Review the minutes.

The secretary should prepare minutes of the prior meeting well in advance; the minutes are one of your key planning tools. Instruct the secretary to get a draft of the minutes to you at least a full week before the meeting you are planning.

Review the minutes to discover any "hot button" issues that were discussed. Were these issues decided by a vote? If so, who is responsible for doing follow through? If you are responsible to contact someone prior to the meeting, be sure to do this. If the secretary was instructed to write a letter, ask if the letter has been written.

Some issues may have been postponed to the next meeting. These issues automatically become unfinished business for the meeting you are planning. Don't omit any of them. Also, if the meeting adjourned in the middle of considering a motion, that motion becomes the *first* item of unfinished business for your next meeting.

Be sure to notice which committees reported and which did not. If a committee failed to report, then it probably should report at the next meeting. If a committee gave an interim report, it may be ready to make a final report at the next meeting.

Pay particular attention to any follow through assignments that were made. Any committee or member who was given an assignment should be held accountable for it at the next meeting. Don't allow important matters to "fall between the cracks." Keep your focus on getting the business of the association done — *all* of it.

Contact key members and committees.

Nobody likes surprises in the middle of a meeting, and it will be unproductive to point to someone who is unprepared and ask for a motion or report. Part of your job is to contact the key people who need to be present to perform specific functions at the next meeting, and be sure they come prepared. You will need to contact your members by any means available, including telephone, postal service, e-mail, fax, or in person. This takes time, but it is your job and no one else can do it for you.

If a committee needs to report at the next meeting, contact the committee chair to be sure that the report will be ready. Find out if the report is only for information or if it contains recommendations for the membership to vote on. Find out if it is an interim report or a final report. If the committee chair wishes other members of the committee to be present, it will be the committee chair's responsibility to contact those members.

If "hot button" issues are coming up, you may need to contact some of the chief spokespersons on the issues to ensure that they are present. It would not be fair to the organization to hear only one side of an issue before taking an important vote. It will be your responsibility to ensure some balance in representation, as well as balance during the actual debate.

Find out which of your officers and other team members will be there to assist you. You don't want to be surprised at the meeting by the sudden discovery that some of your key team members are ill or out of town. You need to know in advance who will be there to assist you in running the meeting.

Prepare an agenda.

Your agenda need not be complex, and it need not be perfect. The agenda that you prepare is only a draft, and the members will have the right to amend it before adopting it. It doesn't become the official agenda until the members have voted to adopt it.

Your draft is important, however, because it provides the basic framework of the meeting. A typical agenda might include the following:

Call to Order
Opening Ceremonies (Pledge of Allegiance, Inspiration, etc.)
Adoption of Agenda
Approval of Minutes
Reports of Officers
Reports of Committees
Unfinished Business (if any)
New Business
Program (if any)
Announcements (if any)
Adjournment

Not all of the above will be included for every meeting. For example, if no business was postponed to the next meeting, and if the agenda of the previous meeting was completed, then you should omit the heading of unfinished business. If no committees are prepared to report, you can simply announce this fact. If there is no planned program and no announcements, these may also be omitted.

Meet with your parliamentarian.

This is probably the most important step of all. Your parliamentarian will review all of the documents pertaining to the meeting including the by-laws, any standing rules or special rules of order, minutes of previous meetings, and your draft of the meeting agenda. Your parliamentarian will help you determine if you have accidentally omitted any important steps in preparing for the meeting, and will help fill in the gaps.

In addition, the parliamentarian will try to anticipate what important motions will be coming up for consideration during the meeting and may assist you and others in drafting these motions. The parliamentarian may also provide a full or partial script to help you get through the most difficult parts of the meeting.

The parliamentarian may also help you develop presiding strategies for handling sensitive issues. For example, you may decide in advance to alternate between speakers for and against a particular motion. You may be able to predict in advance what amendments might be proposed for various motions and decide how you will handle these amendments. The parliamentarian may be able to help phrase a sensitive motion in such a way that no amendments are required.

If you use your parliamentarian effectively, you will never feel that you are alone in handling the meeting. You will regard your parliamentarian as a key member of your team, and you will depend on this person to help get you through any procedural problems. Remember that the parliamentarian's job is to watch procedures, and only procedures. Any time that you feel lost, feel free to lean over to your parliamentarian and whisper, "Where are we now?" You will get a clear, concise answer, and you will be able to keep the meeting moving forward.

Prepare your team.

The final phase of preparation is to ensure that the other members of your team understand their roles in running the meeting. In large organizations, a professional staff does most of this preparation. In smaller organizations, however, much of the responsibility may fall of you.

Some of the types of team preparation that you might wish to consider are as follows:

1. Will you have a timekeeper? If so, are you sure that the timekeeper understands the responsibilities of the job? Will all speakers be timed? Will reports also be timed? Will there be a time limit for considering any single item on the agenda? If so, will points of order and points of information be included in that time? Your parliamentarian can assist you in answering these questions and ensuring that your timer is properly prepared.

2. If key motions on sensitive matters need to be introduced by particular committee chairs or members, are the motions ready? Ideally, you should have a copy of these motions before the meeting begins. Let your parliamentarian review the motions and make suggestions for improving the wording if necessary, so that multiple amendments won't be forthcoming just to clarify the language. You may wish to arrange for some of your officers to introduce key motions.

3. Is anyone going to help you identify which speakers are entitled to be recognized first? You could assign a spotter to do this, but be sure that the spotter understands his or her job. Nothing is more frustrating to members than to be constantly seeking recognition, and never be recognized by the chair.

4. Will motion forms be available to members? If so, where should they pick up the motion forms, and how will these be delivered to the chair? Ideally, all motions should be required to be submitted in writing. The best kind of motion form provides multiple copies automatically to the member moving the motion, the presiding officer, the secretary, and the parliamentarian. You need to ensure that everyone is on the same page, and you will need to repeat the motion frequently for the benefit of members who do not have copies.

This page intentionally left blank.

Chapter 7
Basic Presiding: Main Motions

Most of the business of your meeting will begin with the introduction of a main motion. The main motion is by far the most important motion in all of parliamentary procedure because it is the only motion that is substantive. The adoption of a main motion allows the membership to decide matters of policy or action, to authorize the expenditure of funds, to state the organization's beliefs and priorities, or to express their pleasure or displeasure with occurrences outside the organization. Most of the other motions in parliamentary procedure have little or no substance because they are purely procedural in nature. Motions to adjourn, recess, or close debate, for example, have nothing to do with the substance of what is being considered.

One of your toughest jobs as presiding officer will be to keep the membership focused on matters of substance rather than procedure, and your parliamentarian should help you do this. If you know the proper procedures for handling a main motion, this will help you keep your group's focus where it should be, on the substance of the main motion.

There are not many things in parliamentary procedure that you need to commit to memory, but you should memorize the six steps for handling a main motion. This chapter will help you understand the significance of each step.

Step One: The motion is moved.

A few parliamentary authorities allow discussion of business before a motion is moved, but most authorities insist that business begins with the introduction of a main motion. In order for a motion to be properly moved, three things must happen, and you, as presiding officer, should insist that all three of these things happen in the correct order. This is one of your primary instruments for controlling the meeting.

A member seeks recognition.

The ways in which members seek recognition from the chair is almost infinite. This is an area where custom governs more than anything else. Members may rise and address the chair as "Mr. President" or "Madam President." Members may raise a hand. Members may go to a microphone and press a button or raise a colored card. In some local clubs, "Hey, Joe" may be a sufficient request for recognition. The important thing is that all of the members must accept that they cannot speak or make motions until the presiding officer has recognized them. It is also important that they all agree on the same method of seeking recognition. Confusion will result if you allow some to seek recognition by rising, others by raising a hand, and others by testing the volume of their voice. If necessary, you or your parliamentarian can educate the members regarding the proper method of seeking recognition.

The chair grants recognition to one member.

Granting recognition is one of the presiding officer's most powerful tools for controlling a meeting. Chapter 9 discusses this in more detail. The power to recognize speakers must never be abused. Have you ever seen a meeting where the presiding officer consistently recognized three or four "cronies" and the other members were hardly ever allowed to speak? This is a classic case of abuse and violates the basic rule that no member should be allowed to speak a second time until every member has had the opportunity to speak once.

Don't allow yourself to be rushed into recognizing a speaker and never be bullied into allowing the speaker with the loudest voice to dominate the meeting. Especially when dealing with contentious issues, it is critically important that you recognize the one who is entitled to the floor. If you are in doubt, your parliamentarian can assist you with this, but you should familiarize yourself with the basic rules for recognizing speakers discussed in Chapter 9. Always recognize members in the third person, "The chair recognizes."

A motion is moved.

A member who has been properly recognized may move a main motion by saying, "I move that ...." It is recommended, however, that you not allow a motion to be moved unless you, as presiding officer, have a copy of the motion in your hand. You can avoid a host of procedural problems by insisting that all motions be in writing.

Step Two: The motion is seconded.

To second a motion, a member says, "Second" or "I second the motion." This is one of the few things in parliamentary procedure that does not require recognition by the chair. The only purpose of a second is to ensure that at least two members wish to consider the motion. Neither the mover nor the seconder is required to vote for the motion. Some motions are moved and seconded for the express purpose of creating a record (in the minutes) that the motion was considered and rejected. A motion that comes from a committee does not need a second.

Step Three: The presiding officer states the question on the motion.

This is the "secret" step that most members are unaware of, but it is critical for the correct handling of motions. At this step, the motion changes "property." Before the presiding officer states the question, the motion is the property of the mover. After the presiding officer states the question, the motion is the property of the assembly. This means that, up until the chair actually states the question, the mover can withdraw the motion or change words in the motion because the motion is still his or her property. Once the question has been stated, the motion is the property of the assembly, and the procedures for withdrawing or amending the motion are entirely different.

To state the question, you should simply repeat the words of the motion (reading aloud from the motion form in your hand) and ask for discussion. The first three steps for handling a main motion have now been completed, and the motion is said to be a "pending question."

The general rule is that only one main (substantive) motion can be pending at any given time. Higher-ranking procedural motions may intervene while a main motion is pending, and this concept is discussed in the following chapter. Your parliamentarian will assist you in keeping track of which motions are pending and which are not.

A recommended control technique for the presiding officer is to pause before stating the question on a main motion. Read the motion carefully and see if it makes sense to you. If the motion is written in confusing or ambiguous language, ask the mover to rewrite the motion, not to change its intent, but to clarify the language. This simple technique will often prevent the introduction of multiple amendments, which are very time consuming, and often unnecessary.

Step Four: Discussion

You will be in control of the discussion, and this is where your presiding skills make a genuine difference in the meeting. No one should be permitted to speak without proper recognition. Recognizing speakers during discussion of a motion is one of your most powerful resources for controlling the meeting. Insist that speakers be properly recognized, that they speak only to the chair, and that they limit their remarks to the pending question. When speakers begin talking to each other, wander off the subject of the pending question, or get into personality disputes, you have lost control.

Unfortunately, the power to control discussion is sometimes abused, and the organization suffers. Have you ever witnessed a meeting in which the presiding officer repeatedly recognizes two or three favored individuals while others are unable to gain the floor? This is a sure sign of abuse, and violates the general principle that no member should be permitted to speak a second time until everyone has had the opportunity to speak once.

You will gradually develop your own techniques for ensuring a fair and balanced discussion of issues. One recommended technique is to try to maintain a balance between pro speakers and con speakers so that both sides of an issue are fairly heard. If arguments start to become repetitive, the presiding officer can suggest that speakers limit their remarks to issues that have not already been addressed. If a debate takes up more time than usual, you can tactfully point out other items on the agenda that need to be addressed before adjournment.

Step Five: Take the vote.

Deciding issues by majority vote is one of the fundamental rights of members. The term "majority vote" means more than half of the votes cast. Abstentions should not be counted; abstentions have no effect on the vote. Thus, if twenty-five members are present, and the vote is three in favor and two opposed, the motion is adopted. The fact that twenty members failed to vote has no effect on the outcome.

The presiding officer generally should not vote except on a ballot vote. Your objective is to maintain a position of impartial leadership, and constantly voting publicly on controversial issues will surely imperil your leadership. Nevertheless, there are some instances in which the presiding officer may vote. Any time that the chair's vote will be decisive, you may vote. Thus, if the vote is twelve in favor and twelve opposed, you may vote to break the tie and cause the motion to be adopted. Also, if the vote is twelve in favor and eleven opposed, you may vote in the negative, thereby creating a tie and defeating the motion. Like other members, however, the presiding officer is never required to vote. Some presiding officers prefer to maintain their public neutrality at all times, even on issues about which they may feel strongly.

When you are ready to take the vote, be sure to restate the motion immediately before taking the vote. This is especially important if there has been lengthy discussion and many members may have forgotten the motion.

Most votes are generally taken by voice vote: "All in favor, say Aye. Those opposed, say No." If the vote is close, then you may ask for a rising vote. If the vote still appears close, use your team to take a count. The most important thing is that you never be viewed as "railroading" a motion without taking a fair vote.

Step Six: Announce the result of the vote.

This step appears so simple and obvious that many beginning presiding officers overlook it. The official announcement of the vote, however, is crucial, and much more is involved than simply announcing which side won. A complete announcement of the result contains four essential elements, as follows:

1. Announce which side "has it."

2. Declare the motion adopted or defeated.

   Note: The first two elements are usually combined into a single sentence, i.e., "The ayes have it and the motion is adopted," or "The noes have it and the motion is defeated."

   It is not necessary to announce numbers unless the vote was close. If a count was taken, then you must announce the exact numbers, and these will be entered into the minutes.

3. Indicate the effect of the vote and, if necessary, order that certain things be done to implement the motion. If, for example, a motion has just been adopted to purchase a new computer, the chair's announcement might sound like this: "The ayes have it, the motion is adopted, and the treasurer will solicit bids to be presented at our next regular meeting."

4. If you have an adopted agenda, state the next item of business. This is important because you haven't officially completed one item of business until you have moved on to the next item.

Chapter 8
Basic Presiding: Precedence of Motions

Most parliamentary authorities place a great deal of emphasis on the rules for handling various types of motions. The process can indeed become very complicated. Your parliamentarian, however, can help you through this maze by discretely advising you as the meeting proceeds. Some motions, you will quickly discover, do not require a second; some are not amendable; some are not debatable; some are amendable but not debatable; and some require a two-thirds vote for adoption.

You, as presiding officer, do not need to be concerned about all of these procedural details if you have a competent parliamentarian at your side.

Your presiding, however, will be more consistent and more focused if you at least understand the "principle of precedence." Did you memorize the six steps for handling a main motion discussed in Chapter 7? If not, go back and memorize them now. These six steps are the foundation for understanding how precedence works.

Step four in the handling of a main motion, as you will recall, is "discussion." During discussion, any member, after being properly recognized by the presiding officer, may debate for or against the motion. There are, however, many other possibilities. A properly recognized member may, for instance, give background information on a motion, or the member may choose to make almost any other kind of motion (and there are many to choose from) except another main motion.

How is it possible, you may ask, that a member can make another motion while we are at step four, discussing a main motion? The answer to this is that the main motion has the lowest precedence of all the motions in parliamentary procedure, and therefore will always be voted on last. Any other motion that is introduced during discussion of a main motion (except another main motion) is likely to be in order. You must then work through all six steps of the higher ranking motion before returning to the original main motion.

Assume that we have a pending main motion that "our convention registration fee be set at $100," and this motion is under discussion. Another member, after being recognized, moves to amend the main motion by striking out $100 and inserting $90. The amendment has higher precedence, and therefore we need to go through all six steps for handling the amendment before coming back to the main motion.

If you have those six steps discussed in Chapter 7 firmly in mind, you will know how to process the amendment, using the same six steps. The amendment must be moved, seconded, and stated by the presiding officer. Then discussion will be limited to the amendment. Members may now discuss whether they prefer $90 or $100. The vote is then taken on whether to insert $90 into the main motion, or retain the figure of $100. The result of the vote on the amendment is announced, and we are now back to discussion of the main motion. If the amendment is adopted, we are now discussing the main motion "as amended," which includes the figure of $90.

If you are still confused about the process, this diagram will help you visualize the process for handling a main motion and an amendment.

Stage 1: Original Main Motion

1. I move that our convention registration fee be set at $100.
2. Second.
3. It is moved and seconded that our convention registration fee be set at $100. Is there discussion?
4. Discussion.
   (During discussion, an amendment is moved. Go to stage 2.)

Stage 2: Amendment to Main Motion

1. I move to amend the motion by striking out $100 and inserting $90.
2. Second.
3. It is moved and seconded to amend the main motion by striking out $100 and inserting $90. Is there discussion on the amendment?
4. Discussion.
5. All in favor, say "Aye." Opposed say "No."
6. The amendment is adopted.

Stage 3: Consideration of the Amended Main Motion

1. The pending motion, as amended, is that our convention registration fee be set at $90. Is there discussion?
2. Discussion.
3. All in favour, say "Aye." Opposed say "No."
4. The motion is adopted and our convention registration fee will be $90.

The concept of precedence may be further clarified by the use of "laddering." Envision a ladder of motions with the main motion at the bottom of the ladder. The amendment ranks a bit higher on the ladder. Many other motions in parliamentary procedure can also be amended, and the amendment always ranks higher than the motion to which it is applied. Suppose, for example, that a main motion to sponsor a dance is pending, and an amendment is then introduced to add the words "on February 14." Debate on the amendment becomes lengthy because some members are not ready to make a decision. A member then makes a motion to refer both the main motion and the pending amendment to a committee of three members to be elected. While this motion is being discussed, another member moves to amend the motion to refer by striking out "committee of three members to be elected" and inserting "social life committee." At this point, we have constructed a ladder of four motions. Keeping in mind that each of the four motions must be moved, seconded, and stated for discussion, the ladder may be visualized as follows:

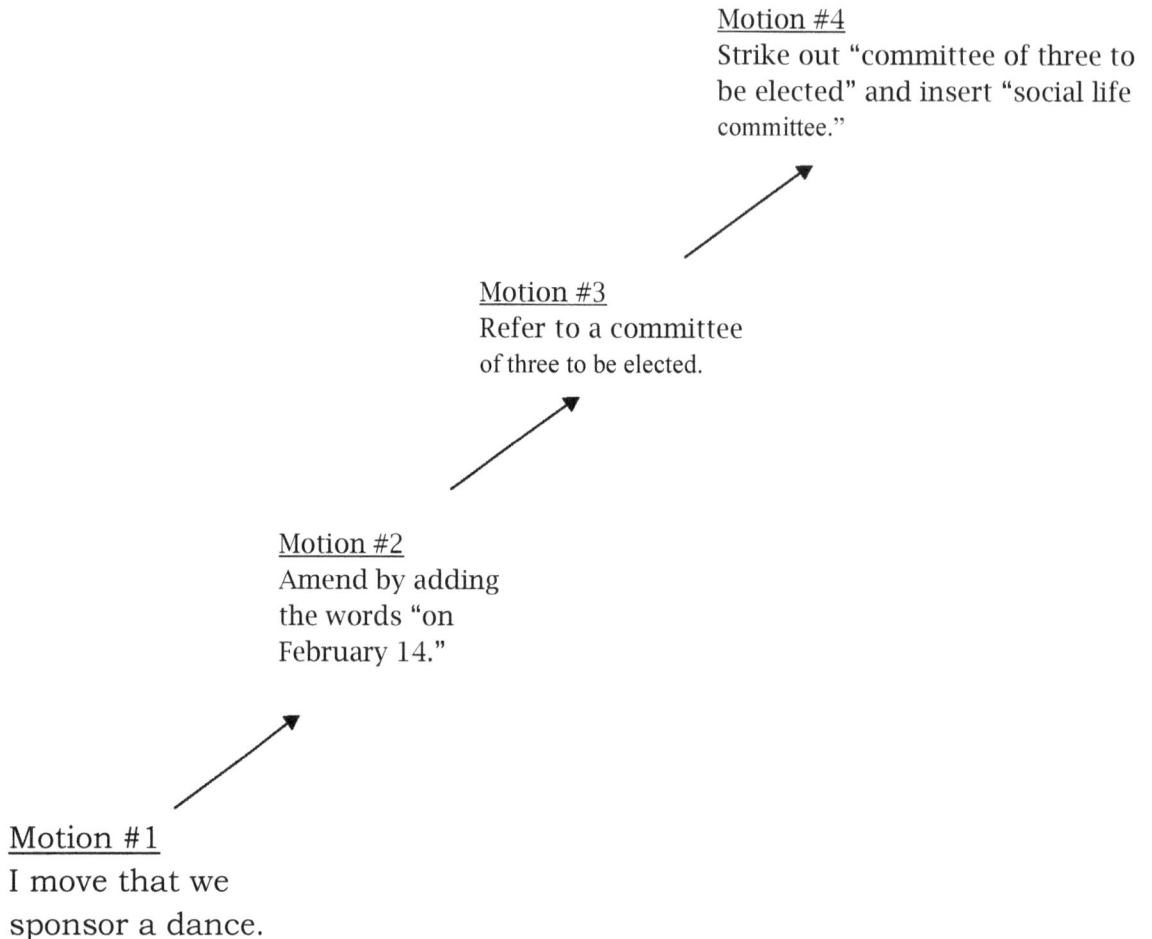

Motion #4
Strike out "committee of three to be elected" and insert "social life committee."

Motion #3
Refer to a committee of three to be elected.

Motion #2
Amend by adding the words "on February 14."

Motion #1
I move that we sponsor a dance.

The motions must be considered in the reverse order that they were moved, seconded, and stated for discussion. The order of voting, then, will be, first, on motion #4, then motion #3, then motion #2, and finally motion #1. The presiding officer's language (with assistance from the parliamentarian) might be as follows:

"The pending motion is to amend the motion to refer to committee by striking out the words 'three to be elected' and inserting the words 'social life committee.' Is there discussion on the amendment? (Pause) We shall now vote on the amendment. All in favor, say *Aye*. Opposed, say *No*. The *ayes* have it and the amendment is adopted.

"The amended motion is to refer the question of sponsoring a dance to the social life committee. Is there discussion? (Pause) We shall now vote on the amended motion to refer. All in favor, say *Aye*. Opposed, say *No*. The *noes* have it and the motion to refer is defeated.

"The pending motion is to amend the main motion to sponsor a dance by adding the words 'on February 14.' Is there discussion on the amendment? (Pause) We shall now vote on the amendment. All in favor, say *Aye*. Opposed, say *No*. The *ayes* have it and the amendment is adopted.

"The pending main motion, as amended, is that we sponsor a dance on February 14. Is there discussion? (Pause) We shall now vote. All in favor, say *Aye*. Opposed, say *No*. The *ayes* have it, the motion is adopted, and we will sponsor a dance on February 14."

One of your parliamentarian's main jobs during a meeting is to keep the ladder of pending motions updated. At any given time, you can consult with your parliamentarian to find out exactly how many motions are pending, and in what order they must be considered. Your parliamentarian can also tell you which motions are not debatable, which are not amendable, which require a two-thirds vote for adoption, and other details pertaining to motions.

Your job, remember, is to keep members focused on discussion of the issues. You do the job of the presiding officer, moving the decision-making process forward. Your parliamentarian will assist you, as necessary, with the procedures.

This page intentionally left blank.

Chapter 9
Basic Presiding: Recognizing Members

One of the most basic rights of members is the right to deliberate on motions before voting. Your job is to ensure that the issues are debated fairly, and that members are recognized in the proper order. Members of your presiding team may assist you in this task, especially for large conventions. For smaller meetings, you may request that your parliamentarian assist you in determining who should be assigned the floor, but many presiding officers choose to do this on their own. To assign the floor properly to a member, you must understand the difference between "standard" recognition and "priority" recognition.

Standard Recognition

To obtain standard recognition, a member seeks recognition through whatever custom is appropriate for the organization. This might consist of rising, raising a hand, saying aloud, "Mr. Chair" or "Madam Chair," or approaching a microphone. Whatever system is used, the member recognizes that, when several members are seeking recognition at the same time, the presiding officer can recognize only one member at a time.

Here are a few basic rules for recognizing members who are seeking standard recognition:

1. Be sure that the member you recognize is a voting member. Generally speaking, the right to propose and discuss motions is restricted to voting members. You should, however, check to see if your organization has special rules regarding the recognition of nonvoting members and guests.

2. Generally speaking, the member first seen or heard to be requesting recognition is the person you should recognize.

3. The mover of a motion is generally entitled to speak first to the motion. If several members seek recognition as soon as the presiding officer has stated the question on a motion, and one of these is the mover, recognize the mover first.

4. A member may speak only twice to a pending motion. If several motions are pending (such as a main motion, an amendment to the main motion, and a motion to refer to committee), a member may speak twice to each of the pending motions.

5. No member should be permitted to speak a second time to a pending question until every member who wishes to speak has spoken once.

6. If the assembly has voted to impose time limits on each speaker, it is the presiding officer's duty to ensure that time limits are enforced. A timekeeper may be assigned to assist the presiding officer.

7. Debate is generally not in order until a motion is pending.

Once a member has obtained the floor through standard recognition, many options are available. The member may speak either for or against the pending motion, or the member may move an amendment or any other higher-ranking motion. A member may have a substantial wait to obtain standard recognition during a very large meeting, but, once having obtained the floor, the member has many options.

Priority Recognition

Priority recognition works in almost the reverse manner of standard recognition. Priority recognition moves the member ahead of all of the other members who may be seeking standard recognition. A member who says "Point of Order," "Request for Information," or some other type of motion of an emergency nature is immediately assigned the floor ahead of other speakers. Priority recognition is therefore easy to obtain but, once having gained the floor through priority recognition, the member does not have the same range of options as a member who obtained the floor through standard recognition.

In very large conventions or annual meetings, it is common to come to the designated microphone to speak or make motions. One of these microphones might be designated specifically for priority motions, and any member approaching this microphone should be recognized ahead of other speakers. Another system in common use is to have monitors at the microphones with colored cards. A monitor who flashes an orange card, for example, might be signaling the presiding officer that the member at that microphone has a priority motion. Whatever system is used, the presiding officer must be quick to recognize a member who seeks priority recognition. At smaller meetings, where microphones are not used, members often gain the floor by simply shouting out "Point of Order" or some similar phrase designating a priority motion.

One of the presiding officer's most important responsibilities is to ensure that priority recognition is not abused. Members who seek to move ahead of other members for the purpose of controlling the floor and entering into contentious debate should be quickly ruled out of order.

A sample list of the most common types of priority recognition:

1. Point of Order. A member who rises to a point of order is indicating that there has been a violation of the rules. In most cases, a point of order can be handled very quickly. If the presiding officer has made an honest mistake in procedure, simply say, "The chair stands corrected" or "Your point is well taken" and announce the correct procedure that you will follow. Points of order may occur in any of the following situations:

    The presiding officer states the question without obtaining a second to the motion.

    The presiding officer calls for debate on an undebatable motion.

    The presiding officer announces that a majority vote will be required for a motion that actually requires a two-thirds vote for adoption.

    The presiding officer recognizes a member to speak a second time on a pending motion while other members who have not spoken are seeking recognition.

    These types of common errors can be corrected quickly. If you make an honest mistake, admit your error and move ahead. Don't assume, however, that you have made an error in procedure every time that someone rises to a point of order. Members who raise points of order are frequently wrong. Suppose, for example, that you have just called for discussion on a main motion and a member rises to a point of order claiming that the motion is not debatable. You will now be required to make a ruling that the main motion is debatable. Your parliamentarian can advise you on detailed procedures for making and enforcing rulings from the chair.

2. Request for Information. A member who rises to a request for information (point of information) is seeking information on the substance of a pending motion. Requests for information are commonly raised immediately before voting because a member may require further information to cast an informed vote. Provided that the question can be answered quickly, the point of information is probably in order. Be very careful, however, that members do not abuse this type of priority motion. Members have been known to gain the floor through a request for information for the purpose of debate. One common device is to ask a five or six part question that initiates a dialogue with the presiding officer. If the question cannot be answered quickly, it is probably not a legitimate request for information and should be ruled out of order.

3. Parliamentary Inquiry. A parliamentary inquiry is the means by which a member seeks procedural advice from the presiding officer. If members are not well educated in the use of parliamentary procedure, the parliamentary inquiry may be their most important means of gaining information about correct procedures. Any of the following may constitute a legitimate parliamentary inquiry:

"What are we voting on?"

"What are we supposed to be discussing now?"

"Would an amendment to the main motion be in order at this time?"

"We've been debating this motion for more than an hour. Isn't there some way that we can move ahead with our agenda?"

When these kinds of questions are asked, the presiding officer is obliged to provide an answer. If you are in doubt, get assistance from your parliamentarian. If the situation is very complex, with many motions pending at the same time, you may wish to have your parliamentarian address the assembly directly.

The above three types of priority motions are only samples of priority motions that allow speakers to be recognized ahead of other members seeking standard recognition. Your parliamentarian can assist you in the proper handling of any matter that requires priority recognition of a member.

The important thing for you to remember is that all priority matters should be handled quickly so that the flow of business is not unduly interrupted. Members who constantly raise multiple points of order and requests for information are probably trying to obstruct the business of the meeting, and should be ruled out of order. You, as presiding officer, are in control of the meeting, and part of your job is to ensure that priority motions don't take control of the meeting away from you.

This page intentionally left blank.

Chapter 10
Basic Presiding: Speaking the Language

Learning to speak the language of parliamentary procedure is much like learning to speak a foreign language. The vocabulary of formal meetings is entirely different from the words that you use in every day speech and, like a foreign language, if you don't use the new language frequently you will lose it. The more you practice speaking the new language, the more comfortable you will be with it. Even so, a new presiding officer has many important matters of substance that may not allow much time for mastering the intricacies of a new language. This chapter will provide a few shortcuts to help you get comfortable with the language of parliamentary procedure as quickly and as painlessly as possible.

Using Scripts

Experienced presiding officers of large organizations commonly read from scripts prepared by the headquarters staff. The parliamentarian should definitely be involved in writing those parts of the script that involve meeting procedures. When bylaw amendments are involved, the parliamentarian may write the entire script.

New presiding officers may perceive that reading from a script weakens their leadership position, but this perception is incorrect. Simply because a script is prepared for you does not mean that you must follow it word for word. Experienced presiding officers often make notes in the margins, indicating specific remarks that they wish to make that were omitted by the staff. The existence of a script also does not prohibit you from announcing an unscheduled recess if you feel that the assembly needs one, or from recognizing the presence of a dignitary in the room who might be making an impromptu visit.

If you are the presiding officer for a small organization, you might consider writing your own script, or inviting your parliamentarian to assist you with writing a script. You cannot, of course, anticipate everything that will occur in a meeting, but many things are predictable. For example, you could certainly write out the language that you plan to use to call the meeting to order, recognize the chaplain for the opening ceremonies, and ask for the reading of the minutes. Even a partial script will help you to relax, knowing that you will be completely comfortable when you come to those parts of the meeting that have been scripted in advance.

In addition to the presiding officer's script, you might consider the advisability of providing scripts for some of your other key officers and committee chairs. A vice president or president-elect who might have to assume control of the meeting in your absence would certainly appreciate a script to work from. If your organization has serious financial concerns, the treasurer might appreciate a script for presenting the treasurer's report. Most of the announcements to be made by the secretary can also be scripted in advance. Committee recommendations and key motions from the floor can be scripted in advance to avoid the necessity of multiple amendments.

Any organization that uses scripts should have at least one script review session prior to the meeting. The officers, the parliamentarian, and key members of the staff should be present for these review sessions. A thorough script review will give you a chance to work out any kinks in advance, and will make your entire presiding team more comfortable as the meeting proceeds.

Using Basic Language

Even though you may not have time to master the complete vocabulary of parliamentary procedure, you should at least learn the most common expressions that you will have to use repeatedly during meetings. Here are some of the most common phrases that you will need.

Procedure	Language
Call to Order	"The meeting will come to order."
Recognizing a member	"The chair recognizes...."
Requesting a second (if necessary)	"Is there a second to the motion?"
Stating the question on a main motion	"It is moved and seconded that (or to).... Is there any debate?" Or, "Are you ready for the question?"
Stating the question and completing action on an amendment to a main	"It is moved and seconded to amend the main motion by adding the word

motion	_____. Is there debate on the amendment? Those in favor say Aye. Those opposed say No. The amendment is (*adopted/lost*). The main motion pending before us is now...
Taking a voice vote:	"The question is on the adoption of the motion to ... Those in favor of the motion, say *Aye*. Those opposed, say *No*."
Taking a rising vote.	"Those in favor of the motion to... will rise. Be seated. Those opposed will rise. Be seated."
Taking a vote by show of hands	"The question is on the motion that.... All those in favor of the motion will raise the right hand. Lower hands. Those opposed will raise the right hand. Lower hands."
Announcing the result of a voice vote	The *ayes* have it and the motion is adopted," or "The *noes* have it and the motion is lost."
Announcing the result of a rising vote or show of hands	"The affirmative has it and the motion is adopted" or "The negative has it and the motion is lost."
Announcing the result for a motion requiring two-thirds for adoption	"There are two-thirds in the affirmative and the motion is adopted," or "There are less than two-thirds in the affirmative and two-thirds for adoption. The motion is lost."
Agreeing to an action by general consent	"If there is no objection to..., the (proposed action) will be taken." Is there any objection to...? (Pause) Since there is no objection, the action will be taken."

Initially, you will need help from your parliamentarian for language dealing with amendments to amendments, appeals, substitute motions, and other more complex motions. With practice, however, you will gradually expand your working parliamentary vocabulary. By the time your term of office is completed, you will be one of the organization's experts on the correct use of parliamentary language.

Learn More Parliamentary Procedure

Don't overlook opportunities to further your own parliamentary education, even though this will not be the main focus of your presidency. The best time to learn parliamentary procedure is *before* you are installed as president. If you are fortunate enough to hold a position of president-elect or vice president who will eventually succeed to the presidency, you have a golden opportunity to acquire knowledge of parliamentary procedure with the relative certainty that you will be using this knowledge very soon.

Many workshops, seminars, and practicums are offered throughout the United States to help people like you. AIP offers at least two practicums per year, one on the east coast, usually in June, and the other on the west coast, usually in late January. Information about the practicums can be found at www.aipparl.org.

You may contact AIP directly to see if there is a chapter of parliamentarians in your area who regularly study and practice parliamentary procedure. Educational materials are sold by AIP and may be viewed on the website. You should also consider taking a course in parliamentary procedure by correspondence. AIP offers several correspondence courses geared to the needs of newly elected officers.

Remember, though, that once your term of office has begun, you will have many other matters to attend to. Your study of parliamentary procedure should commence *before* you have begun your term as president. Always look ahead, and prepare yourself for the possibility that you could soon (perhaps much sooner than you think) be in the position of presiding over the meetings of your organization.

The Presiding Parliamentarian

A few organizations regularly hire "professional presiders" to preside over all of their business meetings. Other organizations hire professional presiders only occasionally for special situations, such as adopting a revision of the bylaws. The professional parliamentarian who acts as the presiding officer does have substantial resources to work with. This person is an expert in the language of parliamentary procedure, and is familiar with many types of complex motions that are unknown territory for most newly elected presidents. The professional parliamentarian also has the advantage of being an outsider with no links to any particular faction or special interest group within the organization.

Professional parliamentarians who preside over meetings, however, lack the elected president's intimate knowledge of the organization's membership, issues, and priorities. Unless the parliamentarian has had extensive experience in working with the organization, this person probably will not understand the full implications of various motions to come before the assembly for consideration. Further, the professional presider will encounter the same dilemma faced by every newly elected president, i.e., how can one person focus adequately on both substance and procedures at the same time? Even the professional presider, to do a good job, will require the assistance of a presiding team.

You, as the elected president of the organization, retain the responsibility for getting the work of the organization done even if someone else does the presiding. In most cases, it is recommended that you prepare yourself for the job of presiding by utilizing the suggestions recommended in this book. If you feel that you are not up to the job and wish to hire a professional presider, be certain that the person you hire has had experience in presiding. Not all parliamentarians are trained to do this. In the end, the organization will hold you responsible for the conduct of your office regardless of who presides during meetings.

This page intentionally left blank.

Chapter 11
Diplomacy from the Chair

Members quickly perceive whether you are trying to be fair in your dealings with members, and they are likely to respond vigorously if they perceive basic unfairness. One of your challenges as a newly elected president is to convince your membership that you genuinely respect the rights of each member and are doing everything in your power to ensure the protection and free exercise of those rights. First, let's discuss what rights your members actually have in a meeting and how you should go about protecting these rights.

Rights of Members

1. *The right to notice of all membership meetings.* Have you ever heard of a meeting in which only certain members were notified that a meeting would occur and other members were not informed? This violates a basic right of members. Members can certainly choose which meetings to attend and which not to attend, but they cannot make an informed choice unless they know when and where *all* meetings are being held.

    Many organizations have regular meeting times that are stated in the bylaws or standing rules. You need not be concerned if your organization has regular meeting times and you are certain that all members know these times. If, however, your meeting times are irregular, it is your responsibility to ensure that members know the time and place of each meeting.

    The bylaws of most organizations also provide that special meetings may be called from time to time. The time and place of these meetings must always be noticed to all of your members, and the notice must also include the exact business to be transacted during the special meeting. Consult your parliamentarian about the wording of the notice for a special meeting. No business will be permitted other than that which is provided in the notice.

2. *The right to speak in debate and to vote on all matters properly brought before the membership.* Members have the right to speak out on any motion before it is brought to a vote, and this right can be limited only by a two-thirds vote. In large conventions, the most common limitation on debate is through the adoption of a special rule of order imposing time limits. When no special rule of order is in effect, your parliamentarian can advise you regarding the proper handling of any motion to limit or close debate on a pending motion.

The manner in which you recognize speakers, discussed in Chapter 9, is the chief means by which you ensure members' rights to speak in debate. You also need to be very careful to take votes in a manner that ensures members' rights are not violated. An inexperienced presiding officer might take a voice vote by saying, "All in favor, say *Aye*. Opposed? The motion is adopted." This careless wording may have deprived some potential negative voters of their right to vote. They weren't told what to say.

An even more careless presiding officer might say, "All in favor, say *Aye*. Well, it's pretty obvious that the motion is adopted." Nothing is obvious when important votes are being taken. You must always take both the affirmative and the negative vote.

The Language of Diplomacy

You, as presiding officer, want to go farther than merely protecting the basic rights of members. You want to be perceived as exercising your authority with due care and diligence, and there are specific techniques that will help you to project an image of basic fairness to your membership.

1. Speak in the third person. You can do this by referring to yourself as "the chair." This may take a bit of getting used to, but it is important. Whenever you say, "The chair recognizes the member" or "The member is recognized," you are speaking in the third person. This keeps the dialogue impersonal. You will need this impersonal language when it becomes necessary to call a member to order.

2. Look for every opportunity to avoid confrontation. Unnecessary confrontations can lead to bitterness, and even lawsuits. If a member attempts to introduce a main motion while a main motion is already pending, avoid saying "You are out of order!" This language only arouses emotions that are unproductive. The diplomatic presiding officer will say, "Your motion is not in order at this time, but it will be in order when we have finished action on the pending motion."

3. Help your members to avoid public embarrassment. You might be surprised how many members sit silently through a meeting simply because they fear any form of public embarrassment. Some members don't want to be on the losing side of a vote for fear of embarrassment. Members often hesitate to present a motion at all for fear that it may be ruled out of order. This is an area where other members of your presiding team can help you out.

   If a particular faction approaches you, your parliamentarian, or any other member of your presiding team to find out whether or not a particular motion would be in order, pay attention. Negotiating in advance of the meeting to find out what the faction really wants can pay off handsomely. Often, with the help of your parliamentarian, you can find out what the faction wants to do and help them develop strategies to do it correctly so that there will be no public embarrassment.

   Nominations for office are sometimes a source of embarrassment. Consider, for example, a faction who wishes to nominate a very popular member for election to an office. The person may not be qualified to run for the office because the bylaws require prior service on the board of directors. You may be in the best position to save both the member and the nominating faction from public embarrassment if the qualifications for nominees are clearly stated at the outset.

4. Respond to parliamentary inquiries with care. Most members don't like to admit their ignorance of parliamentary procedure,

but few of them really know much about it. Educating your membership is, of course, the best answer. Even well educated members, however, will occasionally rise to a parliamentary inquiry during meetings. The last thing you want to do is to give a sarcastic answer that insinuates, "Everybody knows that!" Even if the question seems stupid to you, try to give a positive and thoughtful response, respecting the member's right to obtain a clear answer to the question.

The bottom line is that, to be perceived as fair, you have to do more than protect your members' rights. You also have to ensure that they will be able to speak out and participate freely in meetings without fear of public humiliation or embarrassment. Rulebooks are not very helpful in this area, but protecting their rights is part of your job. You must constantly search for appropriate language that puts your members at ease and encourages them to participate fully in the democratic decision-making process.

Running Hostile Meetings

Meetings that are truly hostile are the nightmare of every presiding officer. You may have done everything in your power to prevent misunderstandings and confrontation. Yet, occasionally meetings do become hostile, and you need to know how to handle these meetings.

When are meetings likely to become hostile? The reasons are almost infinite. Any break from an established custom or tradition, a proposed dues increase, a proposed major change in the bylaws, the creation or deletion of a category of membership, a major expenditure of funds for almost any purpose—any of these, and many more, can lead to major hostility during a meeting.

Your first concern, of course, must be to control your own emotions. If members perceive that you are calm and in control, they are more likely to respect your authority and obey the rules. Your verbal and nonverbal communication will be critical in a hostile situation. If you raise your voice and try to speak louder than the members, this will only aggravate the situation.

If many members are shouting at once, often the best response is to simply wait until there is silence. Then, speak softly and firmly. Your parliamentarian can help keep you focused on the next thing that you should say or do. Keep your remarks in the third person (i.e., impersonal) and keep the tone of your voice low and moderate.

Some presiding officers tend to use their gavel as a weapon during hostile meetings, pounding it loudly and waving it in the air. This is a mistake. The gavel is a symbol of the chair's authority, and should be used very sparingly. A light tap of the gavel to bring the meeting to order, and another light tap to adjourn the meeting are all that is necessary. Abusing your gavel is a sure sign that you are starting to lose control of the meeting.

In a hostile situation, you should frequently remind members that they must address the chair and they must confine their remarks to the pending question. If necessary, state that any remarks of a personal nature will not be tolerated. Your insistence on sticking to the issue at hand is your best defense against losing control of the meeting. Also, remember that a short recess can often provide the necessary "cooling off" period to allow business to continue.

If necessary, your parliamentarian can advise you regarding more extreme measures, such as ordering an unruly member to leave the meeting. Such extreme measures, however, should be your very last resort. Your best defense is to keep your own emotions under control and use tactful, diplomatic language at all times.

This page intentionally left blank.

Chapter 12
Follow Through

Why, you might wonder, should a book on presiding end with a chapter on "follow through"? The answer is that, when the meeting ends, you still have much more work to do. In Chapter 6, we discussed the presiding officer's advance preparation, which often requires more time than the meeting itself. When the meeting ends, it now becomes your job not only to follow through on any tasks that you have been assigned but also to see to it that every officer, committee, and member who was given an assignment performs with the appropriate follow through action.

Follow Through on Minutes

The minutes of the meeting are your best source of information regarding actions that require follow through. Was the secretary instructed to write a letter on behalf of the membership? Then, check with the secretary to find out when the letter was mailed, preferably with a copy to you. Was the treasurer instructed to solicit bids for an expensive purchase? Then, find out when the bids are expected to come in and how they will be reported to the membership. Was the finance committee instructed to draft a new budget for the next fiscal year? Then find out when the finance committee will meet, and whether they have all the information they need to draft a new budget. Did the membership express displeasure with the meeting room? Then, what is being done to improve the situation for the next meeting?

Meetings are held not just to discuss motions, but to take specific actions, and the membership is relying on you to ensure that adopted motions are converted into specific actions to be performed on behalf of and for the benefit of the membership. Following each meeting, you need to find out exactly what follow through is required, who is responsible for doing it, and when it will be done.

The Presiding Officer as Taskmaster

Presidents of organizations sometimes experience difficulty in moving back and forth between the role of impartial presider during meetings and the role of "taskmaster" that must often be performed between meetings. Once the meeting ends, however, the impartial part of your job ends, at least until the next meeting. You are now in the role of an activist leader, overseeing and directing all of the tasks that the members expect to be performed between meetings. At the same time, you are also the "central hub" for communications among the membership. Committee chairs, officers, and staff members will contact you frequently to keep you informed of their progress and perhaps seek your advice on how to proceed to the next step.

Keeping the channels of communication open among your membership not only keeps the organization moving forward, but also helps you prepare for the next meeting.

Your agenda for the next meeting will be the product of the minutes of the previous meeting plus everything that has happened between meetings. You must expect to be at the center of the action for everything that the organization does during your term of office.

Handling Committees

Part of your job is to ensure that important matters affecting the membership don't get buried in a committee. If a particular task was assigned to a committee by the membership, find out when and where the committee will be meeting, who is in charge, and when the committee expects to have a report for the membership. The bylaws of many organizations state that the president is an ex officio member of all committees except the nominating committee. If you are an ex officio member of a committee, this gives you the right to attend and participate actively in all meetings of the committee. Even if you attend only a portion of the committee's meetings, this will enable you to keep track of the committee's progress and predict approximately when the committee will be ready to report.

Wearing Many Hats

Your activist role will vary from one organization to another. Some organizations require their presidents to give frequent speeches in public. Some expect to see and hear their president quoted frequently in the media. Some expect their president to become deeply involved in the details of planning the annual convention. Some presidents are expected to appear in public fundraising efforts on behalf of the organization. Some act as negotiators with sister organizations. Others act as lobbyists for the organization. You will likely wear many different hats during the term of your presidency. Be ready for it, and expect it.

Coordinating Your Team

We have consistently emphasized that presiding is not a one-person job. The follow through phase of your presidency must also be a team effort. Certain things you must do yourself, such as acting as a public spokesperson for the organization or serving ex officio on committees. Other follow through tasks, however, can be assigned to members of your presiding team. If you have a headquarters staff at your disposal, this will serve as the central hub for most follow through actions. Lacking such a staff, other officers must actively assist you.

Some bylaws assign specific roles to vice presidents, such as chairing key committees. If the follow through tasks are not assigned in the governing documents, it becomes part of your job to parcel out assignments and check back to see that each assignment is followed through to completion. Any assigned task that was not followed through to completion should be reported at the next meeting so that the membership can order appropriate remedial action.

Creating a Paper Trail

In addition to everything else that you do for your organization, you must also be concerned that records are kept for all of the things that you are doing. The minutes, of course, are the most important record of what was done during your term of office. If you suspect that the minutes are incomplete or inaccurate, ask your parliamentarian or another member of your team to review them. Minutes can be further refined and amended even after they have been approved. Simply bring them back to the membership at any future meeting and ask for approval of the new amendments to the minutes.

Someone should also be keeping files of news clippings, committee reports, photographs, results of fundraising efforts, and other evidence of what happened during your tenure as president. Records may be kept by the secretary, by a historian, or by the headquarters office. Regardless of where the records are kept, it is part of your responsibility to ensure that these records do not get lost. They are your legacy. They are also an important part of the organization's history.

In future years, you will look back with pride on the many accomplishments of your presidency. You will recall that these accomplishments were not the result of one person's efforts, but of a well-coordinated team that you assembled and directed throughout your term as president. At the moment when all eyes were on you, you mastered the basics of presiding, you discovered that you could actually preside, and

With the help of your team
– YOU DID IT!

www.ingramcontent.com/pod-product-compliance
Lightning Source LLC
Chambersburg PA
CBHW081421270326
41931CB00015B/3359